KIDS CAN COPE

Turn Away from Teasing

by Gill Hasson

illustrated by Sarah Jennings

free spirit
PUBLISHING®

Published in North America by Free Spirit Publishing Inc., Minneapolis, Minnesota, 2020

North American rights reserved under International and Pan-American Copyright Conventions. Unless otherwise noted, no part of this book may be reproduced, stored in a retrieval system, or transmitted in any form or by any means, electronic, mechanical, photocopying, or otherwise, without express written permission of the publisher, except for brief quotations or critical reviews. For more information, go to www.freespirit.com/permissions.

Free Spirit, Free Spirit Publishing, and associated logos are trademarks and/or registered trademarks of Free Spirit Publishing Inc. A complete listing of our logos and trademarks is available at www.freespirit.com.

Library of Congress Cataloging-in-Publication Data
Names: Hasson, Gill, author. | Jennings, Sarah, illustrator.
Title: Turn away from teasing / by Gill Hasson ; illustrated by Sarah Jennings.
Description: Minneapolis, Minnesota : Free Spirit Publishing Inc., 2020. | Series: Kids can cope | Audience: Ages: 6–9 | Summary: "Kids need supportive advice for dealing with teasing—or for knowing when they should stop teasing someone else. This book shares practical tools with kids to help them turn away from teasing. Additional activities are included at the back of the book"—Provided by publisher.
Identifiers: LCCN 2019031719 | ISBN 9781631985287 (hardcover)
Subjects: LCSH: Teasing—Juvenile literature. | Teasing—Prevention—Juvenile literature. | Bullying—Juvenile literature.
Classification: LCC BF637.T43 H37 2020 | DDC 302.34/3—dc23 LC record available at https://lccn.loc.gov/2019031719

Free Spirit Publishing does not have control over or assume responsibility for author or third-party websites and their content.

Reading Level Grade 3; Interest Level Ages 6–9;
Fountas & Pinnell Guided Reading Level N

Edited by Alison Behnke and Marjorie Lisovskis

10 9 8 7 6 5 4 3 2
Printed in China
H13770919

Free Spirit Publishing Inc.
6325 Sandburg Road, Suite 100
Minneapolis, MN 55427-3674
(612) 338-2068
help4kids@freespirit.com
freespirit.com

First published in 2020 by Franklin Watts, a division of Hachette Children's Books · London, UK, and Sydney, Australia

Copyright © The Watts Publishing Group, 2020

The rights of Gill Hasson to be identified as the author and Sarah Jennings as the illustrator of this Work have been asserted in accordance with the Copyright, Designs and Patents Act, 1988.

Series editor: Jackie Hamley

Series designer: Cathryn Gilbert

Turn Away from Teasing

by Gill Hasson

illustrated by Sarah Jennings

It's not always fun to be teased. This book shows how you can deal with it.

It also shows you how to tell when you should stop teasing someone else!

What is teasing?

Teasing is making fun of someone.
It could be making fun of the way someone looks, or the way someone says or does something. It could be making fun of the things someone likes or dislikes.

A person might not mean for teasing to upset someone. Someone might think teasing is harmless and funny. But teasing can become upsetting if it hurts someone's feelings. And if someone asks for teasing to stop but it doesn't, teasing can turn into bullying.

3

What it feels like to be teased

Being teased can leave you feeling embarrassed or ashamed. Your cheeks might burn and you might want to curl up in a ball. Or you may wish you could just sink into the ground.

When you're being teased, you might feel mad.
Your head might fill up with angry thoughts about
things you want to say or do to get back
at the person teasing you.

Feeling bad and missing out

Being teased can also make you feel unsure about things or bad about yourself. You might avoid some activities because you're worried about doing them differently from other people, making a mistake, or getting laughed at.

Ada doesn't like to read out loud in class. Other children tease her because she talks very quietly. Ada feels embarrassed and wants to hide.

Leon doesn't want to play in
the park with his friends because he
feels upset when they tease him about
his shoes being old and cheap.

When you end up in trouble

Sometimes you might feel so angry when someone teases you that you lose your temper. This can end up with you getting in trouble.

Ben teases his sister Annie by copying everything she does, and he won't stop even after she's asked him. Annie gets angry. She shouts at Ben and chases after him. Then Ben blames Annie for chasing him, and she gets in trouble with Mom.

When you get left out

Teasing can be even more hurtful if other people join in with it. Sometimes people tease by leaving someone else out.

Izzy always eats with Emily and Mia at lunchtime, but today they told her she couldn't sit with them. Emily said it was because they were sitting with Evan and Alex to talk about the drama club.

"And *you're* too shy for the drama club!" Alex teased her. Izzy felt really hurt.

Later, Izzy told Mia and Emily that she didn't like being teased for feeling shy, and that they had hurt her feelings by leaving her out.

What can you do about being teased?

One way to deal with being teased is to make a joke of it. If someone teases you, you can laugh and say, "Very funny!"

You might not always feel like you can laugh it off, though. If it makes you feel sad or angry, teasing is not okay.

The good news is that if teasing upsets you, you can do something about it. Sometimes the person doing the teasing might not realize how much it bothers you.

So be sure to tell the person that you do not like being teased and you want the teasing to stop.

How to stick up for yourself

If you are feeling upset or angry because of being teased, remember that there is nothing wrong with YOU!

The person doing the teasing may see it as a game. If you seem upset, the person might keep playing the game. And if you get angry, you might get in trouble. But if you don't react, the game is over.

One way to stop the game is to ignore the person teasing you. If this doesn't work, tell the person that you don't like the teasing and want it to stop. Try not to sound upset. Just speak in a strong voice, loud enough for others to hear. Then walk away and do something else.

The person might keep teasing and try harder to get a reaction. But the less you react, the sooner the person is likely to give up.

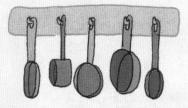

Annie decided to ignore Ben when he copied her. He kept on doing it, so she told him firmly to stop it, loud enough for Mom to hear. Ben didn't want to get in trouble, so he stopped.

Practice speaking up

You could ask someone to help you think of things to say
when you want to stick up for yourself. Then practice!
You can practice with someone else, or by
looking in a mirror, or both. Try saying things like,
"I don't like it when you say that or do that!"
"Stop it!" "That's mean!" or "That's unkind!"

The more you practice, the easier
it will get to speak up calmly and
strongly. Then you'll know just what
to say and do when you need to
stand up for yourself.

I'm a strong person!
I'm a nice person!

When someone teases you a lot, it's easy to start feeling bad about yourself and who you are. You can also practice feeling good about yourself.

Tell yourself that you're a nice, strong person. Think about specific things you like about yourself. Maybe you're a great singer, or good at listening, or a fast runner.

If you start to have sad or bad thoughts, imagine those thoughts sliding straight off you. Then try to think good thoughts and let those thoughts fill your mind.

Talking about being teased

If the people teasing you will not stop, then it's time to talk about it with a grown-up you trust, like a teacher or someone in your family.

When you tell people that you're being teased, they might say things like "just play along" or "don't worry about it." They might tell you that if you do this, the teasing will simply stop.

Sometimes this does work. And if it does, that's great. But if the teasing continues, then getting advice like this is about as helpful as talking to a brick wall!

Getting help

If the person you talk to doesn't help you, talk to someone else you know and trust. This could be a parent, a grandparent, or an older sister or brother. Or it could be a teacher or a friend's parent. Make sure whoever you talk to knows how you feel about the teasing. Tell the person everything that is happening.

This sounds awful for you. Let's talk about what we could do about it.

...and I feel very upset and scared.

Maybe you could ask your teacher to talk about teasing with the class: how it feels, and why it needs to stop when it becomes hurtful.

...and I don't like it.

We'll help you!

Your friends can help too. They could help you tell the people who are teasing you to stop.

If you don't feel you can talk to anyone you know, you can talk to someone on the phone. Look at page 28 to learn more about this option.

Sticking up for others

What if you see someone else being teased or bullied?
What can you do then?

When this happens, you might be afraid that if
you say something, you'll be picked on next. It's important
to keep yourself safe, but if you see someone being teased
unkindly or bullied, there are things you can do to help.
Most people don't like it when someone is mean, and if
you stand up for someone who is being hurt, other
people will probably be on your side.

You could try to stop it by saying something and getting
your friends to speak up too. You could say,
"Don't act so mean!"
If the person does not stop, you or your friends could ask a
teacher or another adult to help.

Two children at school were always teasing Kamil. They called him names and told him that he talked funny. Luisa stood up for him. "It's mean to call Kamil names. Leave him alone!"

When the teasing didn't stop, Josh told the teacher and then asked Kamil to come and play with his group instead.

23

If you tease others

Do you ever tease other people? Maybe you don't realize that you might be hurting their feelings.

One problem with teasing is that it isn't always easy to know when to stop. But if you're teasing someone and the person gets upset or angry, you need to stop immediately and say you're sorry.

Try to imagine how you would feel if someone were doing this to you. You might think that you would just laugh about it, but not everyone can do that.

Look for other ways to have fun without embarrassing or upsetting someone else.

25

When teasing becomes bullying

Teasing can become bullying when it continues after the person being teased has asked for it to stop.

If you tease people in a mean way and you do not stop when they ask you to, then you are bullying them. If you encourage other people to tease someone, or if you don't let someone join in with you and your friends, this is bullying too.

You can't play because you don't know how!

Think about how you would feel if someone treated you this way. If you believe you might be bullying someone, you may need help understanding why and knowing how to stop. Talk to a teacher or family member.

Turn away from teasing

If you're dealing with teasing, here's what you can do:

- Say you don't like it and tell the person teasing you to stop.

- Ignore it as much as you can. Try not to react.

- Stand up for yourself if the teasing does not stop.

- Practice what you will say so the words come easily to you.

- Tell the person firmly, and loudly enough for others to hear, that you want the teasing to stop.

- Stick up for others if you see them being teased. Other people will probably be on your side too.

If you're teasing someone and they get upset or angry, stop immediately and find other ways to have fun. Remember, teasing that upsets someone can become bullying. If being teased is upsetting you, you don't have to deal with it on your own. Tell someone you trust what's happening to you. If you don't feel you can talk to anyone you know, you can call **1-800-448-3000**, text **CONNECT** to **741741**, or go to **yourlifeyourvoice.org** to talk with a counselor. This person will listen to you and give you help and advice about what to do if you're being teased or bullied. You can also go to **stopbullying.gov/kids/what-you-can-do** for help and advice about what to do if you or others are being bullied.

Now you know what teasing feels like ...

... and what you can do to turn away from teasing!

Activities

These drawing and writing activities can help you think more about how to manage teasing and bullying. You could keep your pictures and writing with this book as ideas that can help you cope when you are dealing with someone teasing or bullying you.

- Think of a time when someone has teased you. Draw a picture that shows what happened. At the bottom of the picture, write how you felt about being teased. Which of these words would you use? What other words would you use?
  Hurt, mad, annoyed, irritated, angry, bad, amused, wound up, sad, upset.

- Think of a time when you teased someone else. Draw a picture that shows what happened. At the bottom of the picture, write how you think the person felt about being teased. Which of these words do you think could describe some of those feelings? Is there something you could do to help make things right?
  Hurt, mad, annoyed, irritated, angry, bad, wound up, amused, sad, upset.

- Draw a picture of yourself. Add a speech bubble to the picture and write in it something you'd say to stand up for yourself if you were being teased or bullied.

- Make a big list of things you like about yourself. Look in the mirror and tell yourself these things.

- If you were being bullied or you knew someone else was being bullied, who could you talk to and ask for help? Draw a picture that shows you telling someone.

- Design and create an anti-bullying poster. At the top of the poster you could write the words: No bullying! Then you could write these words (or others that you think of) and decorate the poster with drawings:
  We will not bully others!
  If we see bullying we will:
  Speak up! Get help! Be a friend!

Notes for teachers, parents, and other adults

Most children have experienced being teased by other children or even by adults. Children often feel embarrassed and upset or frustrated and angry about teasing. When children are dealing with being teased, they need to know that it's okay to ask grown-ups for help. Talk with children about the idea that telling a grown-up about mean or upsetting teasing is not telling tales or tattling. Instead, telling an adult about the situation is an important step toward getting help to cope with it.

Children need effective techniques and strategies to help them deal with teasing that is mean or hurtful. *Turn Away from Teasing* explains ways they can do this. The book talks about a number of strategies they can use, and that you can help them with. You can help them learn how to ignore and walk away from teasing, and you can give them ideas for laughing it off if they feel they can do that. You can also help them practice these strategies. The more practice you do in a nonthreatening environment, the easier it will be for children to use the strategies in more high-pressure situations.

What if you're working with a child who is teasing others in a hurtful way? Let children know that this is not acceptable and that it can quickly turn into bullying. Talk with them about why they might be doing this. For example, is there something that's frustrating them and so they're taking it out on other children? Is it possible that they are being bullied by someone else?

If children are being bullied or know someone who is being bullied, it's imperative that they know they can come to you for help. Listen calmly and offer comfort and support. Children may hesitate to tell adults about bullying because they feel embarrassed or ashamed that it's happening, or worry that adults will be upset, angry, or reactive. Sometimes they're scared that if the child who's doing the bullying finds out that they told, the situation will only get worse. Others are worried that adults won't believe them or do anything about it. Or they may worry that adults will tell them to stand up for themselves or even to fight back when they're scared to. Praise children for doing the right thing by talking to you.

Although children can read this book by themselves, it will be more helpful for both of you to read it together. Some children might want to read the book all at once. Others will find it easier to manage and understand a few pages at a time. Either way, you'll find plenty to talk about with children. Ask them questions such as, "Have you ever tried that?" "What do you think of that idea?" "How could that work for you?"

After reading the book and helping children identify some strategies that could work for them, you can come back to the book to remind yourselves of the ideas and suggestions for any future situations. If something didn't turn out so well, talk with children about what they could have done differently. With patience, support, and encouragement from you, children can learn to cope with teasing and better manage their feelings when dealing with being teased. However, if you're concerned that a child is being bullied, it's important to take additional steps. You might intervene in the situation, talk to others about what is happening and how to stop it, and—of course—provide support to the child who is being targeted. It's also extremely valuable to build a safe and supportive environment, to talk with children about kindness and empathy, and to help them learn how to stand up for others.